The Ground of Growth

The "Green Letters" Series . . .

The Green Letters
The Principle of Position
The Ground of Growth
The Reckoning That Counts
Abide Above

The Ground of Growth

The Christian's Relationship to the
Cross and the Risen Christ

Miles J. Stanford

OF THE ZONDERVAN CORPORATION
GRAND RAPIDS, MICHIGAN 49506

THE GROUND OF GROWTH
© 1976 by The Zondervan Corporation

Library of Congress Cataloging in Publication Data

Stanford, Miles J
   The ground of growth,
   (His The "green letters" series)
   1. Christian life—1960-   2. Redemption.
I. Title.   II. Series.
BV4501.2.S7173   248'.4   76-26154

All rights reserved. No portion of this book may be reproduced in any form without the written permission of the publisher.

Printed in the United States of America

CONTENTS

1. Our History in the First Adam 11
2. Our History in the Last Adam 19
3. Diametric Differentiation 27
4. In-Law 35
5. Out-Law 43
6. The World and Its Prince 49
7. Transplantation 57
8. The Process of Conformation 65
9. He Is Our All 73
10. That I May Know Him 81
    Summation 91

PREFACE

In this little handbook we seek to set forth the specific truths of the Cross and the Christ-life as *the ground of growth*. It is our desire that the growing Christian may prayerfully *think* them through, and thereby come to comprehend fully his relationship to the Cross and to Christ risen. This understanding is essential, because of the fact that faith requires a clear concept of truth upon which to focus.

"Meditate upon these things; give thyself wholly to them; that the profiting may appear to all." "The God of all grace, who hath called us unto his eternal glory by Christ Jesus . . . make you perfect [mature], stablish, strengthen, settle you. To Him be glory and dominion forever and ever. Amen" (1 Tim. 4:15; 1 Pet. 5:10,11).

—Miles J. Stanford

Colorado Springs
Colorado

Our History in the
First Adam

Chapter 1
Our History in the First Adam

In this opening chapter we will trace our history in relation to the first Adam: the ruin we received from Adam by inheritance, and the remedy we received from God by the Cross. We cannot become what we already *are* in Christ, until we know what we *were* in Adam. Therefore it is important that we personalize the facts: this is *my* history!

Everything in Adam is the ground of sin and death; everything in the Lord Jesus is the ground of growth and life. Our responsibility is to keep off the old ground, and to live on the new ground — our position in Christ.

The First Adam

To know what we were in Adam we must discover what Adam was, since he is the head of the human race into which we were born. Thus we can understand the nature and condition of the life we inherited from him, the life that continues to indwell us as believers.

Adam sinned and entered death — separated from God, the source of life. Through him we were born into sin, death, judgment, and condemnation. "Wherefore, as by one man sin entered into the world, and death by sin; and so death passed upon all men . . . " (Rom. 5:12). And death not only came into the world and the race, but it reigned as king. "By one man's offense death reigned by one. . . . Therefore as by the offense of one *judgment came* upon all men to condemnation" (Rom. 5:17,18).

Let us note three basic aspects of our relationship to that representative man. (1) Our position of sin (Adam-source); (2) our nature of sin (Adam-nature); (3) our personal sins (Adam-practice). To know the facts concerning the position and condition of our old life in Adam is to possess a vital key to spiritual growth. Ignorance or neglect here means certain defeat throughout one's Christian life.

Our Position of Sin

Because of our fallen progenitor each of us was born into a doomed humanity. As David wrote, "In sin did my mother conceive me" (Ps. 51:5). In Adam, we were declared to be "dead in trespasses and sins," because "in Adam all die" (Eph. 2:1; 1 Cor. 15:22). The result of our position in Adam, our source, is that we are dead unto God, and alive unto sin.

Our Nature of Sin

Our position of sin resulted in a sinful being, or life, and therefore the propensity of that life is sinful. In Adam, we are "*by nature* the children of wrath" (Eph. 2:3; italics mine). In this condition we are natural, fleshly, carnal, separated from God. "The natural man receiveth not the things of the Spirit of God; for they are foolishness unto him: neither can he know them . . . " (1 Cor. 2:14).

This fallen nature never changes, much less improves. "That which is born of the flesh is flesh" (John 3:6). The Adamic nature is self-centered (the sin of sins), therefore totally against God and that irreparably. "For they that are after the flesh do mind the things of the flesh. . . . Because the carnal mind is enmity against God; for it is not subject to the law of God, neither indeed can be. So then they that are in the flesh cannot please God. . . . I am carnal [in Adam], sold under sin" (Rom. 8:5,7,8; 7:14).

Our Personal Sins

The natural product of a sinful nature is sins. The practical result of our congenital condition is stated in Scripture: "All have sinned, and come short of the glory of God" (Rom. 3:23). We grew up to be sinners in practice, and that by choice, hence we were desperately in need of a Savior.

If by careful study of the above we allow the Holy Spirit to impress us with the awful truth concerning our history in Adam, we will be better able to appreciate the wonderful remedy our Father has provided.

THE CONDEMNED ADAM

We must continue to think in terms of our personal history. Now we want to see exactly what our Father did to rectify this terrible relationship and condition.

Our Position of Sin

God did not forgive the principle of Satan-injected sin that dealt the death-blow to the human race through Adam. He does not forgive sin any more than He forgives Satan. On the Cross, in the person of His Son, our Father once and forever dealt with the principle of sin, thereby canceling our position of sin.

"For he hath made him, to be sin for us, who knew no sin." "God sending his own Son, in the likeness of sinful flesh and for sin, condemned sin in the [His] flesh" (2 Cor. 5:21; Rom. 8:3). Far from being forgiven, sin was judged and condemned in death.

Our Nature of Sin

Our sinful life and nature were not forgiven, but likewise were taken into the judgment-death of the Cross. All that we inherited from Adam suffered this same fate. "Knowing this, that our old man was crucified with him" (Rom. 6:6, ASV). Had it been possible for God to forgive our old nature, it could then have been restored, or reinstated.

Our Personal Sins

Our sins were forgiven — past, present, and future — by His shed blood on Calvary. "Who his own self bore our sins in his own body upon the tree." "Having made peace through the blood of his cross." "Unto him that loved us, and washed us from our sins in his own blood" (1 Pet. 2:24; Col. 1:20; Rev. 1:5).

ADAM RELATIONSHIP TERMINATED

At last we can see ourselves at the very end of our history in Adam. On the one hand we look at the Cross, and on the other hand we look into the Tomb. We might ask a few questions as to God's wonderful work in severing us from Adam.

Why? — "The wages of sin is death" (Rom. 6:23). Representative Adam sinned, therefore everything Adamic was condemned to death.

When and Where? — All of God's dealings with sin were accomplished in and by His Son, on the Cross of Calvary.

How? — On the Cross the Lord Jesus was identified with our sin, and our sinful nature, our "old man" being thus condemned and crucified with Him. At the same time, in His substitutionary work of redemption, He paid the penalty of our sins.

Thus His death on our behalf completely freed us, as individual believers, from Adam and all Adamic penalties and consequences. This enabled God to justly include us in Christ's death *unto* sin. "We have been planted together in the likeness of his death. . . . For in that he died, he died unto sin once" (Rom. 6:5,10).

Having by His death borne the condemnation of sin and paid all its penalties, our Lord Jesus died unto, out from, the realm and responsibilities of sin. Stripped of our relationship to Adam by and in that death — we having died in Christ unto the old — we can now see ourselves in His Tomb, ready to be identified with Him in His resurrection life and divine nature.

Let us prayerfully think through these truths concerning our history in Adam, going over them until the Holy Spirit makes the picture clear.

* * * * *

The first step to my becoming free of the old man in daily experience is to know that I was separated once for all from that life by crucifixion and burial. The ultimate in deliverance — death.

Our History in the
Last Adam

Chapter 2
Our History in the Last Adam

Our history in the Last Adam, our risen Lord Jesus, begins on the only basis for resurrection life — death. Our relationship to the first Adam rendered us dead *in* sin, but our death with Christ made us dead *unto* (in relation to) sin — the one condition for newness of life.

IN CHRIST BURIED

There, in the Tomb, we must see ourselves as dead unto Adam, but not yet alive in Christ. Our individual identity has not changed, but our relationship to the fleshly Adam has, thank God! "We were buried therefore with him." "In whom ye were also circumcised with a circumcision not made with hands, in the putting off of the body of the flesh, in the circumcision of Christ [on the Cross]; having been buried with him" (Rom. 6:4, ASV; Col. 2:11, 12, ASV).

Death, our ruin, has been made the very means of our triumph over it. "Death is swallowed up in victory. . . . Thanks be to God, who giveth us the victory through our Lord Jesus Christ" (1 Cor. 15:54, 57).

IN CHRIST RISEN

His death and burial having done its liberating work on

our behalf, we can now begin to look up — from death unto Adam fallen, to birth into Christ risen. When the Lord Jesus burst the bonds of death, He took us with Him in His glorious resurrection life.

"Just as Christ was raised from among the dead by the Father's glorious power, we also should live an entirely new life. For since we have become one with Him by sharing in His death, we shall also be one with Him by sharing in His resurrection" (Rom. 6:4,5, Wey.). Now, safely and forever on resurrection ground in Him, we can study (1) our new position of life; (2) our new nature of righteousness; and (3) our new walk of fruitfulness.

Our New Position of Life

Whereas our old position in the first Adam rendered us dead unto God and alive unto sin, our new position in the risen Last Adam renders us alive unto God and dead unto sin. "For ye died, and your life is hid with Christ in God" (Col. 3:3, ASV). Formerly our Judge, now by means of His Son's death and resurrection He is free to be our Father, and we His sons. "Beloved, now are we the sons of God. . . ." "And because ye are sons, God hath sent forth the Spirit of his Son into your hearts, crying, Abba, Father" (1 John 3:2; Gal. 4:6).

Our New Nature of Righteousness

In our co-resurrection with Christ, our Father gave us a new life with a new nature which can only bring forth righteousness. "Blessed be the God and Father of our Lord Jesus Christ, who, according to his abundant mercy *hath begotten us again* unto a living hope by the resurrection of Jesus Christ from the dead" (1 Peter 1:3).

The old life is not *changed*, but *exchanged* for that which is *altogether new*. Paul's clearest description of this is given in 2 Corinthians 5:17 and 18: "Therefore if any man be in Christ, he is a new creation; old things are passed away; behold, all things are become new. And all things are of God, who hath reconciled us to himself by Jesus Christ. . . ."

Our Father sees each of us as completely new in His Son. We have been forever freed from our relationship to the first Adam with its reign of sin and death. And He wants us to see ourselves from His point of view — new creations in Christ Jesus!

It might be helpful for us to consider further the fact that in this death-to-life transition our personal identity is kept intact. We remain the same individual while acquiring a new position, life, and nature in the risen Lord Jesus. The Father maintains the identity of each believer throughout the process of the Cross, the Tomb, and the Resurrection.

"And *you*, that were sometime alienated and enemies in your mind by wicked works, yet now hath he reconciled in the body of his flesh through death, to present you holy and unblameable and unreproveable in his sight. . . . And *you*, being dead in your sins and the uncircumcision of your flesh, hath he quickened together with him, having forgiven you all trespasses" (Col. 1:21,22; 2:13, italics mine).

In Christ Ascended

Being identified with the Lord Jesus in His death unto sin and His resurrection into life, we are also in Him in His ascended life at the Father's right hand. Born from above, we are to abide above.

"But God, who is rich in mercy, for his great love wherewith he loved us, even when we were dead in sins, hath quickened us together with Christ, (by grace ye are saved;) and hath raised us up together, and made us sit together in heavenly places in Christ Jesus; that in the ages to come he might shew the exceeding riches of his grace in his kindness toward us through Christ Jesus" (Eph. 2:4-7).

OUR NEW WALK OF FRUITFULNESS

As newly created believers, we are in the Lord Jesus in the heavenlies, while at the same time we are in the Spirit of Christ here on earth. The Comforter is our environment in this sin-cursed world. "But ye are not in the flesh, but in the Spirit, if so be that the Spirit of God dwell in you" (Rom. 8:9). He it is who ministers the life of the Lord Jesus in us as our new life, and who develops the characteristics of that life in and through our new nature.

On the one hand, He applies the finished work of the Cross to the life of the flesh within. "Walk in the Spirit, and ye shall not fulfill the lust of the flesh" (Gal. 5:16). On the other hand, He causes the fruit of the Spirit to grow in our new life. "The fruit of the Spirit is love, joy, peace, longsuffering, gentleness, goodness, faith, meekness, temperance" (Gal. 5:22,23).

A close look at Galatians 2:20 may further clarify the distinction between what we were in the first Adam, and who we now are in the Last Adam. "I have been crucified with Christ: and it is no longer I that live, but Christ liveth in me: and that life which I now live in the flesh I live in faith, the faith which is in the Son of God, who loved me, and gave himself up for me" (Gal. 2:20, ASV).

There are vital distinctions here that, when seen, make a world of difference. (1) I, the old man in Adam, have been crucified with Christ; (2) it is no longer the old I that lives, but Christ lives in me, the new creation; (3) the life which I, the new man, now live in the flesh (body), I the new man live in faith; (4) this faith is in the Son of God, who loved me as a lost individual and gave Himself up for me, a sinner.

The oft-quoted words, "Not I, but Christ," tend to give the believer the impression that he as a person is crucified, and out of the picture, and now there is only Christ as his new life. He is wont to feel that he must somehow get himself out of the way, that Christ may be all. Granted, the old self must go down — but the new self must grow up.

It is true that He is our risen life, but it is also true that His is the life and nature of *our* newly created life. "For to *me* to live is Christ." "Christ, who is *our* life" (Phil. 1:21; Col. 3:4, italics mine). We are not to become lost in Him, but He is to be found in us. "That the life also of Jesus might be made manifest in our mortal flesh" (2 Cor. 4:11). He lives in *me*, not instead of me; He is the source and motivation of my Christian life.

* * * * *

I am to realize and rest in the fact that it is *my* being, *my* personality, which is enlifed by the human-divine life and nature of the Lord Jesus. I am the same person, but with a new life in union with His life. By the ministry of the indwelling Holy Spirit *I* will grow in grace and increasingly be conformed to His image.

Diametric Differentiation

Chapter 3
Diametric Differentiation

Let us distinguish yet further between the old life and the new. One important distinction is that sooner or later the healthy believer realizes that he is not alone in his body. The condemned Adam-nature from which he was delivered at the Cross is nonetheless in residence, and as sinful as ever.

Unless we see the extent to which the Cross separated us from the old, we will not be able to keep clear of the enslaving flesh and walk freely in the Spirit. Our Father positionally separated us from the Adam-life by our crucifixion, death, burial, resurrection, and ascension life in the Lord Jesus Christ.

One might ask why our Father, after condemning the old man in the death of His Son, should allow that crucified life and nature to reside in His re-created and risen ones. God has perfect reasons for everything that He does. We can list a few here for consideration.

(1) To reveal the depths of sinfulness from which we were saved.

(2) To teach us to count ourselves dead unto the old, and alive in the new.

(3) To teach us to abide in the Lord Jesus — above.

(4) To teach us to walk in the Spirit — below.

(5) To glorify the Father and manifest the life of the Lord Jesus despite a fallen nature, body, and world.

(6) To give us good cause to watch for His appearing.

(7) To give us a greater appreciation of eternal Glory.

In that there are two distinct natures seeking expression by means of our as-yet-unredeemed body, we must keep them separated in our thinking. In itself the old nature is ever strong to do evil; only by the Spirit is the new nature strong to bring forth righteousness.

THE SPIRIT AND THE OLD NATURE

The sinful nature dooms the sinner, and defeats the believer. The growing Christian is sadly aware of the many ramifications of the flesh that fester within. "Now the works of the flesh are manifest, which are these: Adultery, fornication, uncleanness, lasciviousness, idolatry, witchcraft, hatred, variance, emulations, wrath, strife, seditions, heresies, envyings, murders, drunkenness, revelings, and such like . . . " (Gal. 5:19-21).

The progressing believer not only discovers the characteristics of the fallen nature, but he comes to know and experience its overpowering strength, despite the fact that he is a new creation in Christ. The fallen life within is undergirded by the power of sin, the body, and the world. "I see another law in my members, warring against the law of my mind, and bringing me into captivity to the law of sin which is in my members" (Rom. 7:23).

In time, the defeated believer realizes that the Holy Spirit is the one who is commissioned to deal with the old man. "This I say then, Walk in the Spirit, and ye shall not fulfill the lust of the flesh. For the flesh lusteth [striveth] against the Spirit, and the Spirit against the flesh: and these are contrary the one to the other: so that ye may not [marg.] do the things that ye would" (Gal. 5:16,17).

Although He could do so, the Spirit does not deal with the fleshly life by means of His own strength. He doesn't have to. He depends upon what God has already done about the old man. And so should we. The key to deliverance from the works of the flesh is not strength, as we ultimately learn. Actually, freedom comes by means of explicit faith. As we reckon upon Calvary's crucifixion of the Adam-life, the Holy Spirit applies the finished work to that life thereby holding it in the position of death, inoperative.

The Spirit and the New Nature

While the Spirit draws upon the death of the Cross to render the old nature powerless, He ministers the life of Christ to render the new nature productive. He works according to the principle of life out of death. "For we which live are alway delivered unto death for Jesus' sake, that the life also of Jesus might be made manifest in our mortal flesh" (2 Cor. 4:11).

Only the believer who has repeatedly gone down in defeat under the relentless power of the Adam-nature can appreciate the necessity of walking in dependence upon the Holy Spirit. It is the faithful Spirit who gives growth to our new-creation life, slowly manifesting the very image of its Source. This growth is evidenced by the fruit of the Spirit as set forth in cluster form in Galatians 5:22 and 23.

We might give some thought to the very first segment of that fruit of the Vine, which is *love*. Obviously this love is that of the Lord Jesus; resident in His nature, and therefore in our new nature. We are to behold this love, as well as all the other characteristics of His life, in order that we may intelligently depend upon the Spirit for their development in us. We can look at His love in 1 Corinthians 13:4-13.

"[Love] suffereth long, and is kind; [love] envieth not; [love] vaunteth not itself, is not puffed up,

"[Love] doth not behave itself unseemly, seeketh not her own, is not easily provoked, thinketh no evil.

"[Love] rejoiceth not in iniquity, but rejoiceth in the truth;

"[Love] beareth all things, believeth all things, hopeth all things, endureth all things.

"[Love] never faileth. . . .

"And now abideth faith, hope, [love], these three; but the greatest of these is [love].

"Follow after [love]" (1 Cor. 14:1).

Before considering briefly how to follow after love, we must understand how we are not to walk. What are some of the characteristics of the old nature that we are to shun? It does not suffer long; it is unkind; it envies, vaunts itself, and is usually puffed up. It behaves itself unseemly, seeks its own, is easily provoked, and thinks evil.

This Adam-life within rejoices in iniquity, and does not rejoice in the truth; it refuses to bear all things, believe all things, hope for all things, endure all things. Quite the contrary. And it always fails! Why be occupied at all with that foul brood?

How are we to follow after love? We are to see where God has positioned us, and live there. By means of crucifixion and resurrection our Father has released us from the old life that cannot love, and brought us into union with the life of the Lover. "Your life is hid with Christ in God," "God is love" (Col. 3:3; 1 John 4:8).

As new creations in Christ we no longer have to yield to indwelling sin; the Cross has freed us from its power. But we are responsible to abide in Him by faith, in order that His love and righteousness may be manifested to this needy world. Much of the *how* to escape the old and become established in the new is embodied in Romans 6:11-13 (ASV):

(1) "Reckon ye also yourselves to be dead unto sin, but *alive unto God* in Christ Jesus."

(2) "Let not sin therefore reign in your mortal body, that ye should obey the lusts thereof."

(3) "Neither present your members unto sin as instruments of unrighteousness; but present yourselves unto God, *as alive from the dead*, and your members as instruments of righteousness unto God."

* * * * *

I make choices daily as to what ground I am on: either to be dominated and defeated by indwelling sin, or to be freed and growing in the Lord Jesus Christ. There can be no neutrality. The Lord Jesus has made it very clear: "No man can serve two masters; for either he will hate the one, and love the other; or else he will hold to the one, and despise the other. . . . He that is not with me is against me" (Matt. 6:24; 12:30).

In-Law

Chapter 4
In-Law

The believer will remain in bondage as long as he does not know that through the Cross he has been delivered from the reign of the old man, the law, the world, and the Enemy. We have already discussed the Adam-life. In this chapter we will deal with the law, both as commandment and as a principle.

Purpose of the Law

Strictly speaking, God's formal Law was given to the nation Israel and to none other. The following points will clarify its place and purpose.

(1) Four hundred and thirty years before God introduced the Law, He gave Abraham the covenant of promise. This covenant had to do with faith, and with Christ.

Faith – "Abraham believed God, and it was accounted to him for righteousness. . . . So then they who are of faith are blessed with faithful Abraham" (Gal. 3:6,9).

Christ — "Now to Abraham and his seed were the promises made. He saith not, And to seeds, as of many; but as of one, And to thy seed, which is Christ" (Gal. 3:16). The Father's Old Testament expression of His one and only way of salvation was by grace through faith in the coming Messiah.

(2) Over four centuries after Abraham received the covenant of promise, God presented the Law to the Jews.

"For the law was given by Moses" (John 1:17). The Law was not meant to replace the principles of promise, grace, and faith, but was brought in alongside. "The law, which was four hundred and thirty years after, cannot disannul, that it should make the promise of none effect. For if the inheritance be of the law, it is no more of promise; but God gave it to Abraham by promise" (Gal. 3:17,18).

(3) God's "law is holy, and the commandment holy, and just, and good" (Rom. 7:12). But it has to do with sin and death, not righteousness and life. "For by the law is the knowledge of sin" (Rom. 3:20). The law reveals man's condition and intensifies his need. "But sin, that it might appear sin, working death in me by that which is good; that sin by the commandment might become exceedingly sinful" (Rom. 7:13).

(4) The Law can have nothing to do with grace, or faith, or life. "No man is justified by the law in the sight of God. . . . The just shall live by faith. And the law is not of faith. . . . But before faith came, we were kept under the law, shut up unto the faith which should afterwards be revealed. Wherefore, the law was our schoolmaster until [marg.] Christ, that we might be justified by faith" (Gal. 3:11,12,23,24).

The Law and The Old Nature

The Law has to do with sin, and therefore it applies to the Adam-life, the old man.

(1) The ministry of the Law is to judge and condemn all that came from Adam. "The law is not made for a righteous man, but for the lawless and disobedient, for the ungodly and for sinners. . . ." "For when we were in the flesh [Adam], the [sinful impulses], which were [aroused] by the law, did

work in our members to bring forth fruit unto death" (1 Tim. 1:9; Rom. 7:5).

in our members to bring forth fruit unto death" (1 Tim. 1:9; Rom. 7:5).

(2) The fleshly Adamic nature will have nothing to do with God, nor can God have anything to do with it. He used His Law to judge and condemn it to death. "For the mind of the flesh is death . . . because the mind of the flesh is enmity against God; for it is not subject to the law of God, neither indeed can it be" (Rom. 8:6,7, ASV).

THE CHRISTIAN AND THE OLD NATURE

The old man, whether Jew or Gentile, is under law. For the former, it is external, via command; for the latter it is internal, via principle. "For when the Gentiles, which have not the [external] law, do by nature the things contained in the law, these, having not the law, are a law unto themselves" (Rom. 2:14). The old nature is law-oriented; carnal, not spiritual.

The Christian who is mainly living by means of the old life, and thereby giving expression to the old nature, is carnal, fleshly. (The Latin word for carnal is *carnis*: flesh.) Hence whether by command or by principle, the law is predominant in his life. He is under law as a rule of life; he is in Romans Seven.

Results of Law – Negative:

(1) The law says, Don't sin, so he struggles to keep from sinning. The law says, Do righteousness, so he struggles to be righteous. But the law does not give the Christian power over sin — it gives sin power over the Christian! "The strength of

me. . . . For the good that I would, I do not; but the evil which I would not, that I do" (Rom. 7:21,19).

(2) The Christian who is walking after the flesh is walking under law, and therefore is doomed to failure. Law applies to the fleshly life, but there is no good thing in that nature; it is neither subject to the law, nor can it be (Rom. 7:18; 8:7). The carnal believer is depending upon fleshly means for deliverance from fleshly failure; he is looking for strength to the very source from which he is seeking deliverance.

(3) The Christian life becomes a burden, and a continuous up-and-down experience. There is little hunger for the Word of God. Prayer all but fades away. Sins are not honestly confessed, hence there is scarcely any true fellowship with the Lord. Instead of having a testimony and being a pattern, such a defeated believer becomes a detriment to others. What love he has is self-centered — there is none for the needy. Instead of manifesting the love of the new man in Christ, there is the opposite expression from the old man in Adam — unkindness, envy, unseemly behavior, and other works of the flesh.

(4) As to service, where there is any at all it is mainly by means of self-effort — whether it be preaching, teaching, or personal witness. Flashy gimmicks and neat little methods are employed, but the flesh can only spawn more of its own kind. The problem is compounded.

From time to time there may be a bit of reviving in the life by means of dedication, but this usually results in deeper frustration and depression. There is no growth or fruitfulness for the believer in the legal realm. To such Paul says, "Ye are yet carnal: for whereas there is among you envying, and sin is the law" (1 Cor. 15:56). "I find then a law [indwelling principle] that, when I would do good, evil is present with strife, and divisions, are ye not carnal, and walk as [natural] men?" (1 Cor. 3:3).

Results of Law – Positive:

Through all this legalistic and fleshly failure, the Father is working out His eternal purposes. He is using the principle of law to bring the believer to the end of Romans Seven: "Oh, wretched man that I am!" Thus the Christian is prepared for the wonderful exchange of faith — that of turning from the old law-bound nature to his new life of grace in the Lord Jesus. By the Spirit he will be brought from the realm of the [old] law of sin and death into that of the [new] law of the Spirit of life in Christ Jesus (Rom. 8:2).

* * * * *

By various maxims, forms, and rules,
That pass for wisdom in the schools,
I sought my passions to restrain;
But all my efforts proved in vain.
But since my Saviour I have known
My rules are all reduced to One,
To keep my Lord by faith in view,
This strength supplies and motive too.

—*John Newton*

Out-Law

Chapter 5
Out-Law

If a Christian is under the law as a "rule of life," he is laboring in a doleful, gray, alien land of self-righteousness — he struggles to produce. The believer who learns to walk in the Spirit of life in Christ Jesus has the joy of the Lord for his strength — he rests to receive.

Instead of our Father demanding *from* us according to the law, by grace He ministers *to* us from the One who is our life in glory. "And God is able to make all grace abound toward you; that ye, always having all sufficiency in all things, may abound to every good work" (2 Cor. 9:8).

THE LAW AND THE NEW NATURE

Our new nature is that of the risen life of the Lord Jesus Christ. The purpose of the Law being to reveal sin and condemn the sinner, it has nothing to say to the new man in Christ Jesus. "For sin shall not have dominion over you; for ye are not under the law, but under grace" (Rom. 6:14).

(1) As each of us was separated from the Adam-life by means of the Cross and the Tomb, we were delivered from the realm of law. We rose from the Tomb into newness of life — out of the grip of law into the freedom of His resurrection. "Now we are discharged from the Law and have terminated all intercourse with it, having died to what once restrained and held us captive. So now we serve not under [obedience

to] the old code of written regulations, but [under obedience to the promptings] of the Spirit in newness [of life]" (Rom. 7:6, Amp.).

(2) Law has to do with works — the works of the flesh. The new creation has to do with life — the life of the Son. Abiding in Him, our nature will grow and manifest the fruit of the Spirit. "You have undergone death as to the Law through the [crucified] body of Christ, so that now you may belong to Another, to Him Who was raised from the dead in order that we may bear fruit for God" (Rom. 7:4, Amp.).

THE CHRISTIAN AND THE NEW NATURE

Our Lord Jesus Christ, seated at the Father's right hand in glory, is not under law of any kind. His life is subject neither to commands nor to the principle of law. It is holy by nature. We, having been born into Him, now share His life. "For to me to live is Christ . . ." (Phil. 1:21).

(1) The wages of sin being death, the law by the execution of the death penalty exhausted its rights over the man in Adam. Having died unto the law in Christ, the law no longer has any *claim* on the believer. He is now free from its reign. "When the commandment came, sin lived again, and I died — was sentenced by the Law to death." "For I through the law died unto the law, that I might live unto God" (Rom. 7:9, Amp.; Gal. 2:19, ASV).

(2) Being in Christ Jesus, the believer no longer has *need* for the law as a governing principle — he can now live by nature, effortlessly and naturally. "We are debtors, but not to the flesh — we are not obligated to our carnal nature — to live [a life ruled by the standards set up by the dictates] of the flesh" (Rom. 8:12, Amp.).

(3) When the believer sees his deliverance from the old, he can begin to walk in the freedom of the new. "Where the Spirit of the Lord is, there is liberty." "For, brethren, ye have been called unto liberty; only use not liberty for an occasion to the flesh . . ." (2 Cor. 3:17; Gal. 5:13).

WALKING IN LIBERTY

Some of the positive results are the following:

(1) Even when there is failure, the abiding believer learns from it and gains thereby. He knows that his Father is working all things together for his good, to conform him to the image of His Son (Rom. 8:28,29). His reliance is neither upon the law nor the flesh, but upon the Holy Spirit, "that the righteousness of the law might be fulfilled in us, who walk not after the flesh, but after the Spirit" (Rom. 8:4).

(2) Instead of struggle to keep from sinning, and self-effort to progress spiritually, he rests in Christ — the ground of growth. The Word of God is his daily sustenance; he feeds on it in reliance upon its Author, the Spirit of Truth.

(3) Prayer is his cherished fellowship with the Father; he depends upon the Spirit for this most vital aspect of his life. "The Spirit also helpeth our infirmities; for we know not what we should pray for as we ought; but the Spirit himself maketh intercession for us with groanings which cannot be uttered. And he that searcheth the hearts knoweth what is the mind of the Spirit, because he maketh intercession for the saints according to the will of God" (Rom. 8:26,27).

(4) Having learned to hate the old life, he willingly judges himself. He confesses his sins fully and without fear because he loves and trusts his Advocate and Redeemer, the Lord Jesus Christ.

(5) In his growth he is more and more free from the influence of indwelling sin and the old life, the law, and the surrounding world. He is at rest concerning himself, but burdened for others. His service is from the heart and in the Spirit — a sharing of *life*. He does not have to resort to human methods and fleshly means to win others and help them grow in grace and in the knowledge of the Lord Jesus. He allows the Holy Spirit to control and work through him by means of life — the life of the Lord Jesus.

(6) Underlying whatever service the Spirit may lead him into, his most important and effective ministry is simply to *be* — for to him to live is Christ. He becomes an "example (pattern) for the believers [and the lost], in speech, in conduct, in love, in faith and in purity" (1 Tim. 4:12, Amp.). His attitude is that of Paul, "Stand fast therefore in the liberty wherewith Christ hath made us free, and be not entangled again with the yoke of bondage [law]" (Gal. 5:1).

* * * * *

My liberty from the old is infinite in the Lord Jesus — limited only to the glory of my Father, and to the good of others.

The World and Its Prince

Chapter 6
The World and Its Prince

Continuing the consideration of that from which Christ has freed us, this chapter will deal with two of our deadly enemies, the world and Satan.

The World

Satan is the god and prince of this present evil world system (John 12:31; 2 Cor. 4:4). The world is the chief weapon by which he ever seeks to cripple the Christian. "For all that is in the world, the lust of the flesh, and the lust of the eyes, and the pride of life, is not of the Father, but is of the world." "The whole world lieth in the evil one" (1 John 2:16; 1 John 5:19, ASV).

The Worldly Christian

It is in the environment of this world that the Adam-nature is at home and flourishes. The believer who is dominated by the old nature is bound to be worldly. He feels that he can live for God effectively on a carnal level. He imagines that such a manner of life and service will attract the world to the unworldly Savior.

Others go to the opposite extreme by attempting to live for God through legalistic measures. But this is resorting to the wrong realm of life. "If then you have died with Christ to material ways of looking at things and have escaped from the world's crude and elemental notions and teachings of externalism, why do you live as if you still belong to the world? — Why do you submit to rules and regulations? [such as], Do not handle [this], Do not taste [that], Do not even touch [them], referring to things all of which perish with being used. To do this is to follow human precepts and doctrines.

"Such [practices] have indeed the outward appearance [that popularly passes] for wisdom, in promoting self-imposed rigor of devotion and delight in self-humiliation and severity of discipline of the body, but they are of no value in checking the indulgence of the flesh — the lower [old] nature. [Instead, they do not honor God] but serve only to indulge the flesh" (Col. 2:20-23, Amp.).

Fleshly means are futile, whether utilized to win the world, or to avoid the world.

> Whatever passes as a cloud between
> The mental eye of faith and things unseen,
> Causing the brighter world to disappear,
> Or seem less lovely, or its hope less dear,
> This is our world, our idol, though it bear
> Affection's impress, or devotion's air.

The Christ-centered Christian

The risen Lord Jesus is the abiding-place and environment of our new nature, and it is in that life we are to walk, "for our citizenship is in heaven" (Phil. 3:20, ASV).

It is there, abiding above, that we fellowship and grow; and it is from there that we minister here in this lost and needy world. Although we are in this world, we are not of it; we are primarily here in order for God to be glorified in us and the Lord Jesus to be manifested through us for the sake of others. "Conduct yourselves properly (honorably, righteously) among the Gentiles, so that although they may slander you as evil doers, [yet] they may by witnessing your good deeds [come to] glorify God" (1 Pet. 2:12, Amp.).

To escape from the reign and corroding influence of the world we must count on the work of the Cross, by which we were crucified unto the world, and the world crucified unto us (Gal. 6:14). The source of our Christian life is neither in the worldly nature, nor the worldly system; we are to look to another world for all our resources. "If [since] then ye were raised together with Christ, seek the things that are above, where Christ is, seated on the right hand of God. Set your mind on the things that are above, not on the things that are upon the earth. For ye died, and your life is hid with Christ in God" (Col. 3:1-3, ASV).

Satan

Both the Cross and the risen Lord Jesus separate us from the reign of Satan. At Calvary we died out of his kingdom of darkness and death; in the resurrection we were born into the Son's kingdom of light and life. "Giving thanks unto the Father, who hath made us meet to be partakers of the inheritance of the saints in light; who hath delivered us from the power of darkness, and hath translated us into the kingdom of his dear Son" (Col. 1:12,13).

Resist

Satan would seek to bluff us out of our position of safety. But we are to "be sober, be vigilant; because your adversary the devil, as a roaring lion, walketh about, seeking whom he may devour; whom resist steadfast in the faith. . . ." "Neither give place to the devil." "Submit yourselves therefore to God. Resist the devil, and he will flee from you" (1 Pet. 5:8,9; Eph. 4:27; James 4:7).

Our resistance to the Enemy is on the basis of faith, faith in the work of the Cross in which he was doomed and his power broken. Through our reckoning, his defeat at Calvary is applied and we are made to triumph.

Satan, although dangerous, has been defeated. "For this purpose the Son of God was manifested, that he might destroy the works of the devil." "Forasmuch then as the children are partakers of flesh and blood, he also himself likewise took part of the same, that through death he might destroy [make of no effect] him that had the power of death, that is, the devil" (1 John 3:8; Heb. 2:14).

Stand

We are to stand in our position, "hid with Christ in God," that we may be "strong in the Lord, and in the power of his might" (Col. 3:3; Eph. 6:10). We do not have to wage war with the devil to obtain our position, nor do we have to fight him either to maintain it or to retain it. We simply stand where we have been placed, abiding above, resisting his assaults and fiery darts through faith in the Victor who defeated him and all his cohorts. At the Cross the Lord Jesus "spoiled principalities and powers, he made a shew of them openly, triumphing over them in it" (Col. 2:15). We humbly walk in the train of His triumph.

Rest

Many believers, not knowing of, nor abiding in, their

position in the triumphant Lord Jesus, attempt to war against and defeat the devil and his demons. Before long Satan looms larger and stronger in their eyes, while the Lord Jesus seems to become smaller and weaker.

Soon they imagine there are demons on every hand, possessing nearly everything and everybody. They become obsessed with their "warfare," and before long begin to experience defeat and breakdown in the physical, mental, moral, and spiritual realms.

If Satan can get the believer to become more aware of him than of the Lord Jesus, the inevitable result is a triumphant foe and a defeated Christian. Our responsibility is to steadfastly resist the Enemy by quietly resting in our impregnable position in Christ. "For in him dwelleth all the fulness of the Godhead bodily. And ye are complete in him, which is the head of all principality and power." "Let us therefore cast off the works of darkness, and let us put on the armour of light" (Col. 2:9,10; Rom. 13:12).

Our Father often uses the Enemy as a foil, to teach us to handle our weapons of defense. We are told to "put on the whole armour of God, that ye may be able to stand against the wiles of the devil" (Eph. 6:11). Actually, the Lord Jesus is our armor — "put ye on the Lord Jesus Christ, and make not provision for the flesh" (Rom. 13:14). Satan cannot touch Him, nor can he touch us in Him.

Even when our Father chooses to let out Satan's chain a bit, the Enemy's worst only proves to be God's best for the believer who stands his ground in Christ. Satan thought he was destroying the Lord Jesus on the Cross, and now he attempts to do the same with the believer. But all he gets is a mouthful of ashes, his Calvary defeat. All he gets is judgment, "because the prince of this world is judged" (John 16:11).

* * * * *

I am thankful that the Cross has closed my history as related to the world and its prince. I was a slave to the world, but now it is crucified to me, and I to it (Gal. 6:14). I was a slave to Satan, but now my Father has made me a partaker of the inheritance of the saints in light, and delivered me from the power of darkness (Col. 1:12,13).

Transplantation

Chapter 7
Transplantation

We would seek to encourage the believer by explaining the way in which our Father uses the old sinful life to establish us in the new righteous life. By faith we stand in the work of the Cross for the Spirit's opposition to all that would hinder our growth, and by faith we abide in the Lord Jesus for the Spirit's accomplishment of that growth. We stand, and He works.

Downward Progress

Before we can "grow up into him in all things, which is the head, even Christ" (Eph. 4:15), there must be a growth downward; a good root system must be established. Both naturally and spiritually, the underlying development comes first. The superstructure is dependent upon a solid subterranean foundation.

Usually the believer is awakened and enhungered for true spiritual growth by an increasing awareness of the virulence and power of the old nature. Most Christians struggle for years in the vain attempt to control indwelling sin. The result is an up-and-down, defeated spiritual life.

A portion of 2 Corinthians 4:11 can give us valuable light here: "Alway delivered unto death." One of the most effective but heartrending applications of this death in the life of the believer is his realization of the sinfulness and strength of the flesh. The story of the reign of this death-dealing nature overcoming the believer is titled "Romans Seven."

Sooner or later the Christian discovers that, despite the fact he is a new creation in Christ, he has not the strength to overcome this sin nature that would ruin his life and testimony. On and on goes the losing battle, year after weary year. "For I fail to practice the good deeds I desire to do, but the evil deeds that I do not desire to do are what I am [ever] doing" (Rom. 7:19, Amp.).

LIBERATING LIGHT

But in time, God's time, the Holy Spirit begins to enlighten the failing believer as to the real truth about the reign of sin. "Now if I do that I would not, it is no more I [as a new creation] that do it, but sin that dwelleth in me" (Rom. 7:20). This enlightening is the beginning of the end of the reign of sin in the believer.

The awakened Christian realizes that he does not have to submit to the indwelling source of sin, and that it is now an alien realm to him. He has a new sphere of life in which to abide. He can submit to the old source, he can choose to walk in its ways, he can by carelessness be overcome by its power — but he need not, and should not.

Some of the believer's sinful cooperation with the old nature is due to his inability to distinguish clearly between the workings of the old and those of the new. But sad failure teaches him to recognize, and repudiate, the old man for what it is. His realized need develops his discernment and appreciation of the Lord Jesus' life within.

TURNING POINT

The Holy Spirit uses the pressure and process of death within to prepare for the development of the resurrection life.

The believer sees that the sin and carnality so often experienced is being produced by the old nature — certainly not by the new.

He begins to value his freedom to reject the sin-producing nature via the work of the Cross, to reckon himself to have died unto the old man. Death now separates the old from the new. "For we are the circumcision [separated from the flesh], who worship God in the spirit, and rejoice in Christ Jesus, and have no confidence in the flesh" (Phil. 3:3).

This should be an encouragement: Our growing hatred of the works of the flesh ultimately causes us to stand clear in our liberated position in Christ. He gives us freedom by means of the Cross, and growth by "the law of the Spirit of life." Now we know who is who! "That which is born of the flesh is flesh; and that which is born of the Spirit is spirit" (John 3:6).

The old man will never change. It will ever be sinful and produce nothing but death, hence it must neither be cultivated nor coddled. We are to have nothing to do with the old, and everything to do with the new. "For neither is circumcision [now] of any importance, nor uncircumcision, but [only] a new creation [the result of a new birth and a new nature in Christ Jesus]" (Gal. 6:15, Amp.).

Everything apart from our new life has been fully dealt with and condemned at the Cross. Thank God, we are new creations in Christ Jesus! Old things are passed away (in death), and all things are become new (in Christ) — these are the two basic truths that we are to lay hold of. We have been freed from the old and can turn from it to give our full love and attention to Him who is the source of the new (2 Cor. 3:18).

It is normal for the believer to want to grow up in the Lord Jesus, to become more like Him. But he does not at first realize how much his upward development depends upon a deep and solid root system. This the Spirit accomplishes by making us aware of the fleshly life within, and the sin of our alliance with it.

By such negative means He brings us to the place of humility. Thus we learn the necessity of complete dependence upon the Spirit of God, the Son of God, the Word of God, and our Heavenly Father who is the Husbandman. We are being rooted and grounded for growth.

Upward Progress

When the Holy Spirit has our root system well enough established, when we begin to exercise faith in the put-down of the old life by the Cross, and when we learn enough of the sin and danger of trafficking with the Adamic life, *then* it is that He turns our faith to the True Vine. "And hath raised us up together, and made us sit together in heavenly places in Christ Jesus" (Eph. 2:6).

In general, Christians focus upon the death of the Lord Jesus — He died for me. But for the growing believer, His life must be the focal point of faith — "Christ, who is our life." His is a "justification of life" (Col. 3:4; Rom. 5:18).

Emphasis upon His death gives assurance of the new birth, but what the believer needs is growth. Growth comes from life, resurrection life. "That I may know him, and the power of his resurrection" (Phil. 3:10). My position is in Him at the Father's right hand, and it is there that I find life and fellowship. Christians who dwell mainly upon His death know little of life — His life.

Looking upon Him as our life, the Holy Spirit enables us to exchange the old for the new. "And have put on the new man, which is renewed [recreated] in knowledge after the image of him that created him." "That ye put on the new man, which after God is created in righteousness and true holiness" (Col. 3:10; Eph. 4:24). In this risen position, hidden and resting in the Lord Jesus, I am on the ground of growth, free to grow up in Him. "My little children, of whom I travail in birth again until Christ be formed in you" (Gal. 4:19).

> Dead and crucified with Thee, passed beyond my doom;
> Sin and law forever silenced in Thy tomb.
> Passed beyond the mighty curse, dead, from sin set free;
> Not for Thee earth's joy and music, not for me.
> Dead, the *sinner* past and gone, not the sin alone;
> Living, where Thou art in glory on the Throne.

*   *   *   *   *

If I selfishly cultivate the old ground there will be nothing but a grim harvest of wood, hay, and stubble, "for he that soweth to his flesh shall of the flesh reap corruption . . ." (Gal. 6:8).

If I sacrificially cultivate the new ground there will be an eternal life-giving harvest, for, "unless a grain of wheat falls into the earth and dies, it remains [just one grain; never becomes more but lives] by itself alone. But if it dies, it produces many others and yields a rich harvest" (John 12:24, Amp.).

The Process of Conformation

Chapter 8
The Process of Conformation

While the ground of growth is celestial, the realm of the development and manifestation of that growth is terrestrial. We are to abide in our Lord Jesus there, in order to grow and become fruitful here — branches in the inverted Vine.

In the foregoing chapters we have sought to establish the ground of truth upon which we are to stand. Now we need to see how that truth is made practical in our daily life and service. But let us first mention three of the principal reasons why many believers fail to live in the new life that is theirs in Christ.

Lack of Knowledge

The most prevalent factor is that many Christians do not know the truth concerning their union with the Lord Jesus in His death, burial, resurrection, and ascension. All know about His substitution *for* them, but too few realize their identification *with* Him. This is mainly due to the fact that the identification truths have long been a neglected teaching in schools, churches and homes.

Misapplied Knowledge

There are others, less numerous, who do know their participation in this aspect of the work of the Cross. However, after reckoning upon their identification with Christ, they set about to produce its results by self-effort.

It is not readily understood that only the Holy Spirit can make experiential in us that which is already true of us in Christ. It is His specific ministry to apply the death of the Cross to the old man, and develop the life of the Lord Jesus in the new man. Our responsibility and privilege is to exercise faith in the facts of our identification and to walk in (dependence upon) the Spirit of life in Christ Jesus (Rom. 8:1,2). "Walk and live habitually in the (Holy) Spirit — responsive to and controlled and guided by the Spirit; then you will not gratify the cravings and desires of the flesh" (Gal. 5:16, Amp.).

Unbalanced Knowledge

Still others are saying in their hungry hearts, "I know now that I died to the old nature on the Cross of the Lord Jesus, and I confidently reckon upon that liberating truth. But I am not so clear about the second half of the reckoning. I seem to know more about the work of the Cross than I do about my new life in the risen Christ."

Be encouraged! Take one thing at a time. The Cross comes first: death to the old precedes the manifestation of life in the new. The years of struggle and failure have not been wasted, but have been governed by His loving hand to prepare the hungry heart for the blessed exchange. By means of His processing there comes a time when the failing believer begins to realize that living in and relying upon the old nature is *sin*, not just a disappointing inconvenience.

Living in the old Adam-life is illegal cohabitation; it is spiritual adultery. The believer has been "married to another, even to him who is raised from the dead, that we should bring forth fruit unto God" (Rom. 7:4). He has to learn that in the old fleshly nature "dwelleth no good thing," and that even its so-called "righteousnesses are as filthy rags" (Rom. 7:18; Isa. 64:6).

Exchange

This all-important realization provides the necessary hatred of the old man, and the desire not for change but for *exchange*. The horrible old relinquished for the holy new! But what about this life in Christ Jesus? In Him we are totally recreated, not just new creatures. Remember that in the Tomb we were *dead*. Then in Christ risen we were totally regenerated, not just renovated. A butterfly is a new creature, not a new creation. But our new life and nature are a completely new creation of God. "All things are become new. And all things are of God" (2 Cor. 5:17,18).

Knowing the Old

When the Christian's knowledge of Christ as his new life is insufficient or in error, he more or less abides in the old nature because that is the best he knows. How tragic! His mind and his life are centered in that sphere. Is that not just where most believers are today? They are woefully aware of the sinfulness of the old life within, but they are hung up right there. Even so, the Holy Spirit sees to it that this realm of existence becomes unbearable.

The work of the Cross has enabled them to be free from the domination of the old man, yet they are still paying attention to it. The more they dwell on that source the more it is activated — and its one by-product is "no good thing," nothing but sin. They must let the truth of their position overwhelm the feelings of their condition.

KNOWING THE NEW

When the old life within becomes intolerable, it is time to become acquainted with the new. "O unhappy and pitiable and wretched man that I am! Who will release and deliver me from [the shackles of] this body of death? O thank God! — *He* will! through Jesus Christ . . . " (Rom. 7:24,25, Amp.).

There is the key — knowing the new! It was not for nought that John said, "And this is life eternal, that they might know thee, the only true God, and Jesus Christ, whom thou hast sent." Nor that Paul exclaimed, "That I may know him . . . " (John 17:3; Phil. 3:10).

How do we come to know Christ as our very life? It is by the Word, and that by the Spirit. The Lord Jesus said, "I am . . . the truth." He said to His Father, "Thy word is truth." And He said of the Holy Spirit, "When he, the Spirit of truth, is come, he will guide you into all truth" (John 14:6; 17:17; 16:13).

If we leave the realm of the Spirit-wrought-and-taught Word of truth in an effort to know Christ more personally, some seeming "angel of light," some denizen of the dark, or an overheated imagination will have us thrilling over a "Jesus" who is not the Christ. Many today are thus led astray.

Then too, for many Christians their knowledge of God, and their attitude toward Him, are based upon and controlled by circumstances — and/or their personal condition — rather than by the Word of God. They judge Him by what they feel He is doing for them, or seemingly is not doing for them. Self-centered, they complain and flounder from failure to failure.

But when our knowledge of our Father is Bible-based, we are able to evaluate our circumstances and personal condition in the light of who He is. Then there is rest and joy in Him no matter what the situation may be. To know Him is to trust and love Him. Calvary is the proof of His love for us, even if there were no other indication or if all other indications were to the contrary. "Whom he did predestinate, them he also called: and whom he called, them he also justified: and whom he justified, them he also glorified. What shall we then say to these things? If God be for us, who can be against us? He that spared not his own Son, but delivered him up for us all, how shall he not with him also freely give us all things?" (Rom. 8:30-32).

It is natural for the believer's mind to become fixed upon the old nature within, because that has always been his life. But now it is sin to do so. He has a new life and nature, and a renewed mind. And he has been freed from the old so that he can dwell upon and abide in the new. To think in the realm of the old brings forth sin and death. To think upon the new results in righteousness and life.

Paul, in the Word of Truth, exhorts us, "Finally, brethren, whatever things are *true*, whatever things are *honest*, whatever things are *just*, whatever things are *pure*, whatever things are *lovely*, whatever things are of *good report*; if there be any *virtue*, and if there be any *praise*, *think on these things*" (Phil. 4:8, italics mine). Actually, all of these "things," in their highest essence and reality, are centered in the life of our Lord Jesus Christ.

* * * * *

As I rely upon what the Cross has already done with the old man, I am free as a new man to become intimately acquainted with the Lord Jesus. I am thereby resting in the very process that conforms me to His image.

He Is Our All

Chapter 9
He Is Our All

Think of the closer-than-breathing, bone "of his bones" (Eph. 5:30) relationship of life we have with the very Creator and Sustainer of the universe. Although He is seated in glory at our Father's right hand, He is not far off — His life is in us where we are, and our life is in Him where He is. Absolute oneness. "He that is joined unto the Lord is one spirit [with Him]." "For we are his workmanship, created in Christ Jesus. . . . Now in Christ Jesus ye who once were far off are made nigh . . . " (1 Cor. 6:17; Eph. 2:10,13).

He Is Our Head

When we see Jesus Christ as the sovereign Lord of the universe, we acknowledge Him to be the ruler of our personal lives and our circumstances. He is our Head; we are His body on earth. Our Father "hath put all things under his feet, and gave him to be the head over all things to the church, which is his body, the fulness of him that filleth all in all." "He is the head of the body, the church: who is the beginning, the firstborn from the dead; that in all things he might have the preeminence. For it pleased the Father that in him should all fulness dwell" (Eph. 1:22,23; Col. 1:18,19).

He Is Our Intercessor

The better we know the Lord Jesus in His glory, the more fully will we depend upon Him as our personal Intercessor. "Wherefore, he is able also to save them to the uttermost that come unto God by him, seeing he ever liveth to make intercession for them." "Who shall lay any thing to the charge of God's elect? It is God that justifieth. Who is he that condemneth? It is Christ that died, yea rather, that is risen again, who is even at the right hand of God, who also maketh intercession for us" (Heb. 7:25; Rom. 8:33,34).

When the believer sins, his relationship to the Father is not affected, but his fellowship with Him is impaired. It is for this self-induced exigency that we need the Lord Jesus at the Father's right hand as our Advocate and Intercessor. He is Jesus Christ the righteous, our defender in heaven against all the accusations of the Adversary. Since we have been "made the righteousness of God in him" (2 Cor. 5:21), He justly and continually clears us from all charges. And because He "of God is made unto us . . . righteousness" (1 Cor. 1:30), He is never our prosecutor.

When we fail to confess our sins, or to judge ourselves in the matter of sin, we must be chastened. When our Father's child-training is applied, it is always well deserved and for our good. Our Lord Jesus bore all the wrath against sin on the Cross, therefore we grow by means of the chastening. "Now no chastening for the present seemeth to be joyous, but grievous; nevertheless afterward it yieldeth the peaceable fruit of righteousness unto them which are exercised thereby" (Heb. 12:11).

There are many Christians who feel that confession of sin is unnecessary. They reason that if their sins are already fully forgiven, why bother to confess them? It is true that we need not ask for forgiveness when we sin; rather, we are free to thank Him for that forgiveness provided at Calvary and received in Christ. But it is necessary to honestly confess our sins, thus siding with Him against ourselves, else how can we enjoy true fellowship with the One who is holy and hates sin perfectly?

The primary ministry of the Holy Spirit is to reveal to us the Lord Jesus as our new life, and to occupy our minds and hearts with Him. When we step down into the old life and consequently sin, the Spirit is grieved and must occupy us with ourselves until our honest confession of sin to the Father brings restoration of fellowship.

Yes, frank and immediate confession of sin is vital. Think for a moment of someone who observes a loved one sinning against him. Wounded, but ever loving, he forgives and says nothing. Meanwhile the loved one, although knowing there is forgiveness, does not confess his sin. Forgiveness is there, love is waiting. But now where is the fellowship and integrity of this relationship?

"But if we walk in the light, as he is in the light, we have fellowship one with another, and the blood of Jesus Christ his Son cleanseth us from all sin. If we say that we have no sin, we deceive ourselves [not Him], and the truth is not in us. If we confess our sins, He is faithful and just to forgive us our sins, and to cleanse us from all unrighteousness" (1 John 1:7-9).

He Is Our Life

By now we should be seeing more clearly the wonderful truths concerning the fact that the Lord of glory is our Life, and that we are, as individuals, new creations in Him. There is but one place, one position, where we are to abide and that is in Him where He is. The resources and motivations of our daily lives are in the Son who is seated at the right hand of the Father. The expression of our new lives here is the indwelling life of Jesus manifested in our mortal flesh.

Our position and our resources as new creations are certainly not in the old man. Our death on the Cross now and forever separates us from the reign of sin, and we are free to reckon upon that fact. Our mind does not have to dwell upon and become involved with the indwelling sinful nature — death is there; life is in the Lord Jesus.

We are looking in the wrong direction, whether we dwell upon the old man and are pulled down in depression and defeat by its sinfulness, or conversely consider that nature to be quite harmless and good. We have to slip past the Cross and violate our identification with Him in His death unto sin, in order to traffic in that realm. Paul asks, "We who died to sin, how shall we any longer live therein?" (Rom. 6:2, ASV).

Our position as new creations is not in this sin-cursed world. We are traveling through it, but not abiding in it. How is it that the growing believer can rest and be at peace in the midst of this world of death, free to hold forth and share the Word of life? It is simply because his anchorage and source of life is in another Person in another world. Keep looking down!

The death of the Cross stands not only between us and the old nature, but also between us and this world system. "But far be it from me to glory, save in the Cross of our Lord Jesus Christ, through which the world hath been crucified unto me, and I unto the world" (Gal. 6:14, ASV).

There is nothing here for us to rely upon; there is everything there for us to depend upon. On earth, death; in glory, life. "For if while we were enemies we were reconciled to God through the death of His Son, it is much more [certain], now that we are reconciled, that we shall be saved [daily delivered from sin's dominion] through His [resurrection] life" (Rom. 5:10, Amp.).

If today the roots of your life are in the old nature, and therefore in the world, absorbing the poison and death of those Cross-condemned sources, it is time to move! There is a quiet and restful abiding place just where our Father has positioned us. Our communion is with the Father and the Son, where they are.

Is it not time to hide from the old by hiding in the new? In that attitude of faith and walk of fellowship our Lord Jesus will have another life through which to reach and replenish others. Therefore, "if any one preaches, let it be as uttering God's truth; if any one renders a service to others, let it be in the strength which God supplies; so that in everything glory may be given to God in the name of Jesus Christ, to whom belong the glory and the might to the Ages of the Ages. Amen" (1 Pet. 4:11, Wey.).

* * * * *

Fellowship with the old life results in nothing but sin, and chastening; fellowship with the Lord Jesus results in love, and life for others.

That I May Know Him

Chapter 10
That I May Know Him

Our object in sharing these truths of the Word is that we may be turned *from* all that God condemned *unto* a deep personal knowledge of our Lord Jesus Christ. Truth can be very impersonal and ineffective if its ultimate purpose is not realized. What we need is the Spirit's application of the full-orbed work of the Cross. This will enable us to avoid the sin within and without, and to give our complete attention and love to the Lord Jesus. Anything short of this will satisfy neither Him nor the hungry heart.

We must remember that it is by learning to know the Lord Jesus that we know our Father. "Have I been such a long time with you, and yet hast thou not known me . . . ? He that hath seen me hath seen the Father. . . . Believe me that I am in the Father, and the Father in me . . . " (John 14:9,11).

We are not to know the Lord Jesus in order to emulate Him as our example. Rather we are to behold Him in the Word and allow the Spirit of God to conform us to His image. Not imitation, but conformation. If we flounder in the old man and pay attention to his clamorings, the hateful works of the flesh will inevitably be manifested for all to see and suffer from.

Our Lord Jesus said, "Learn of me" (Matt. 11:29). His infinite glory must not discourage us from pursuing our privilege of knowing Him intimately. His divine majesty is unfolded in order to display His divine mercy. To encourage the reader's further study, let us behold Him from several different viewpoints.

His Life as Creator

The Word sets forth Christ as He was prior to His humiliation here on earth, in the glory which He had with His Father before the world was (John 17:5). There He is seen as Creator, in one aspect of His life. God does nothing directly, but all through His Son and by His Spirit. That is why it was in the Lord Jesus that He created us anew. "For by him [Christ] were all things created, that are in heaven, and that are in earth, visible and invisible, whether they be thrones, or dominions, or principalities, or powers — all things were created by him, and for him" (Col. 1:16). Thus we can come to know Him as *Creator*.

His Life on Earth

"The fruit of the Spirit" is developed in us as we behold Him in His earthly walk and work. For actual growth, there is to be an entering into His life via the Word — feeding upon Him, appropriating Him.

(1) Consider the Lord Jesus as He lovingly shares His life with the up-and-out religious leader, Nicodemus, and the down-and-out woman of Samaria. Listen closely to Him. Observe His tender concern for these individuals who represent the extremities of the spectrum of human need. Note how faithfully and effectively He applies the truth to their hungry hearts; not by method, but by

nature — a ministry of *life*. Study John 2:23–3:21, and 4:5-26.

(2) Pay close attention to Him as He calls His first four disciples, and especially note the way He ministers to Peter. Study Luke 5:1-11. Spend time with Him as He shares and applies His wonderful parables by the sea. Study Matthew 13:1-58. Enter into His restful attitude as He in turn gives rest to the tossing tempest and the tempest-tossed. Study Mark 4:35-41.

(3) Stand with Him as He commissions the Twelve; observe Him; listen to what He shares with them. Study Matthew 9:36–11:1. All of this teaches us who He is and what He is like. Feed upon Him as He feeds the four thousand, and hear Him reveal Himself as the Bread of Life. Study Mark 8:1-9; John 6:22-71.

(4) How touchingly His character is depicted in His parable of the Good Samaritan. Study Luke 10:25-37. And nowhere is He more explicitly manifested to us than in His fellowship in the Bethany home. Study Luke 10:38-42; John 11:1-46. And what of His humble yet ever majestic service to the Twelve during the Last Supper? How our love is drawn out to Him there! Study Luke 22:7-30.

These are but a few of the specific instances in the Word by which we can come to know Him more intimately. Thus we realize something of the life the Holy Spirit is developing within *our* hungry hearts.

His Life in Glory

The Holy Spirit does not limit us to the earthy, nor to the earthly life of the Lord Jesus. Knowing Him in His humility is preparation for knowing Him in His glory. Remember the

Lord Jesus' prayer, "Father, I will that they also, whom thou hast given me, be with me where I am, that they may behold my glory . . . " (John 17:24). We are to behold Him as He was and know Him as He is, so that we may be like Him here and now.

We come to know Him as He is from the vantage point of our position in Him at the Father's right hand, and this ever by means of the Word. Our Father "hath raised us up together, and made us sit together in heavenly places in Christ Jesus" (Eph. 2:6). By intelligent and confident faith we are to abide above in our life-source. "If then ye were raised together with Christ, seek the things that are above, where Christ is, seated on the right hand of God. Set your mind on the things that are above, not on the things that are upon the earth. For ye died, and your life is hid with Christ in God" (Col. 3:1-3, ASV).

As we behold His glory there, we are conformed to His humility here, "that the life also of Jesus might be manifested in our mortal flesh" (2 Cor. 4:11). Abide above to grow below. The Lord Jesus set the pattern: "He that came down from heaven, even the Son of man which is in heaven" (John 3:13). It is true that the source of our Christian life is in His glory, but *that* aspect of our lives will not be revealed until His appearing. "The glory which thou gavest me I have given them." "When Christ, who is our life, shall appear, *then* shall ye also appear with him in glory" (John 17:22; Col. 3:4).

First humility, then glory; first the Cross, then the Crown. Is it not worth waiting for? We are "heirs of God, and joint heirs with Christ; if so be that we suffer with him, that we may be also glorified together. For I reckon that the sufferings of this present time are not worthy to be compared with the glory which shall be revealed in us. For the earnest expectation of the creation waiteth for the manifestation of the sons of God" (Rom. 8:17-19).

What a comfort, as we study to know Him better in His glory, to be assured that the Father will honor Paul's faithful intercession on behalf of each one of us: "That the God of our Lord Jesus Christ, the Father of glory, may give unto you the spirit of wisdom and revelation in the knowledge of him; the eyes of your understanding being enlightened; that ye may know what is the hope of his calling, and what the riches of the glory of his inheritance in the saints" (Eph. 1:17,18). Whose inheritance?

HIS LIFE AS RULER AND SUSTAINER

Not only did our Lord Jesus create and redeem, but He ever upholds that which is His. Not only is He the Sustainer of the universe which He created, but He also coordinates and directs all within the realm and unto the consummation of His Father's eternal purposes — and that includes each of His own. "God . . . hath in these last days spoken unto *us* by his Son, whom he hath appointed heir of all things, by whom also he made the worlds; who, being the brightness of his glory, and the express image of his person, and upholding all things by the word of his power, when he had by himself purged *our* sins, sat down on the right hand of the Majesty on high" (Heb. 1:1-3).

The late Dr. Wm. Graham Scroggie made this observation which gives us further reason for rejoicing in the Lord Jesus and having no confidence in the flesh (Phil. 3:3):

Our understanding of Nature, and our interpretation of History, are both partial and faulty; yet, if we are Christians at all, we must believe that back of both is the Divine Thinker, the Infinite Wisdom, and the Almighty Power, Who is the Son of God our Redeemer and Life.

Things have not been started and then left to run on their own material or moral momentum, but all things are under the constant control of the Divine Creator, in Whom all things have their center of unity, Who appoints to everything its place, Who determines the relation of things to one another, and Who combines all into an ordered whole, so that this Universe is a cosmos and not chaos.

It is not law ultimately which rules this Universe, but God our Father, and He rules it through His Son our Saviour. Human history is not in the grip of fate, but in the hands of Him Who was pierced for *us* on Calvary.

His Life Our Ground of Growth

The ground of the first Adam is that into which we were born and in which we grew. It is there that the world, the flesh, and the devil would keep us in bondage. It is the ground of carnality, sin, and death — off-limits to the new creation in Christ.

The ground of the Last Adam is that into which we have been reborn and are to abide. It is there that the Father, Son, and Holy Spirit would have us grow and mature. It is the ground of spirituality, righteousness, and life — the Father's one abiding place for the believer.

As we take our rightful stand on the resurrection side of the Cross, setting our minds and hearts on the Lord Jesus via the Word, the Holy Spirit will establish us in Him above. On that ground of growth, we will "grow in grace, and in the knowledge of our Lord and Saviour, Jesus Christ. To him be glory both now and forever. Amen" (2 Pet. 3:18).

Summation

Summation

The following quotation from a message by Norman F. Douty seems to sum up what we have been seeking to share.

> When we say that Christ's life has come into us to displace ours, what do we mean? We do not mean that this life of the Lord Jesus has come in to displace our personality. When I speak of our fallen life, I do not mean the human personality as such. I mean the poison which permeates our personality, the poison of sin which has degraded and defiled and distorted our humanity.
>
> It is not that this new life of the Lord Jesus comes in to take the place of our personality, to take the place of our faculties created by God, but it comes in to take the place of the sinful life which is operating in our personality and employing our faculties. The vessel is the same, but the contents are different — the same vessel, the same person, the same faculties, but the contents different. No longer this sinful element, but the very holy nature of the Lord Jesus Christ filling, interpenetrating, permeating.
>
> Our Father is not seeking to abolish us as human beings and have the Lord Jesus replace us. He is seeking to restore us as human personalities so that we may be the vehicle through which Christ will express

Himself. Therefore you find that whenever God gets hold of a man, instead of abolishing his personality, He makes it what He intended it to be.

Redemption is the recovery of the man, not the destruction of the man. And when the Lord Jesus in us is brought to the place He is aiming for, there will not be an atom of the old life left, but the *man* will be left — glorified in union with the Lord Jesus Christ.